COME WALK WITH ME

An Introduction
to the
Mass
and the
Catholic Faith

Carl Turner

ISBN: 1479203335
ISBN-13: 9781479203338

ACKNOWLEDGEMENTS

I would like to give a very special thanks to Father Denzil Vithanage without whose guidance, encouragement and inspiration this book would not have been possible.

I would also like to thank my wife Diane for all her help and suggestions throughout the development of this book and for being my companion and spiritual inspiration for all these years.

COME WALK WITH ME

CONTENTS

COME WALK WITH ME

FOREWARD

The Mass is at the heart of the Catholic faith. It is a family meal where Catholics engage the present and recall and relive when Jesus walked the earth. Like most families who have pictures of their ancestors around, Catholics also have pictures of their ancestors, the saints, around in the form of statues and stained glass. The Mass brings us all together and it is here that Jesus gives himself to us and we become one with him. It is here that Jesus reminds us that we are all indeed one family and that we are to love God and one another lest we forget. Catholics seek this family gathering wherever in the world they find themselves for the Mass is everywhere.

Welcome to the Mass!

⌘

1 EARLY ONE MORNING

It was early morning and I was standing in a grassy field with more than a half a million young people who had come there from all over the world. The day before they had walked over five miles to this large open field in Toronto, Canada. During the misty and windy night they had slept in the open in sleeping bags, makeshift tents and some on simple tarps. Their dress, their speech and the make up of their campsites revealed that every language and culture of the world was represented. While I was standing there it suddenly became so quiet that you could only hear the rustling of the breeze, which was remarkable considering that there was a sea of youth that spread as far as the eye could see.

That morning there had been plenty of noise as the multitude sang and praised God. Then there was scripture reading and now everyone was quiet in order to hear the homily. But whom were they waiting to hear? Was it a rock star? Was it a preacher who would give an emotional impassioned sermon in an effort to reach them? No, it was a very elderly man that had to be helped onto the stage and into his chair. He sat leaning over his table and with some considerable effort spoke slowly but clearly. Many of the youth wore headsets so they could hear what he had to say in their own language even though he used six different languages during his message.

Pope John Paul II always spoke to their hearts and they all knew it as they listened intently. However John Paul was not the main reason they had come. They had come together for a Mass. When it was time for the Eucharist, out of nowhere appeared Nuns who approached each person, lifted up the host and looked at them and said, "The Body of Christ." Within a short period of time more than a half a million young people had received the Eucharist.

What is it about the Mass, I wondered, that had attracted so many young people? What is it about this ceremony that had such great appeal to each generation despite the fact that it had remained relatively unchanged for two thousand years? Why has the Mass today captured the hearts of over one billion people or one sixth of the world's population and why is it that somewhere in the world a Mass is being held every minute of every day?

I had been a Catholic for nearly twenty years and I knew I would never have all the answers. I knew I could not understand the Mass completely just as I could not fully understand Jesus or the ones I love. There are mysteries here that my finite mind simply cannot completely surround.

But the Mass that day grabbed my heart just as it had when I first became Catholic and in my own mind I knew why. It is in the Mass that Jesus loves me so much that he gives all of himself to me, his Body, Blood, Soul and Divinity. The Mass is where I encounter Jesus physically as well as spiritually. During that one hour or so time has no meaning and Jesus asks us actually to step back two thousand years and be with him as were the apostles. And for that hour Jesus also asks us to join with the angels in their worship of God.

Each Mass is an exciting journey in time and space and I had discovered that at every Mass Jesus looks at us and says, "Come walk with me." That is what this book is about.

⌘

2 A STEP BACK IN TIME

The Mass is not only a step back in time with Jesus but it is also a step back in time with the first Christians as they gathered for worship. Few realize that we know about their worship. Both Peter and Paul went to Rome establishing the Christian communities and suffering martyrdom there. Persecution of the Christians continued and in 155 AD the emperor of Rome asked St. Justin to write down what Christians did in their well-established worship services thus giving us the first detailed description of early Christian worship that can be found in paragraph 1345 of the Catechism of the Catholic Church.

The Mass of all ages

1345 As early as the second century we have the witness of St. Justin Martyr for the basic lines of the order of the Eucharistic celebration. They have stayed the same until our own day for all the great liturgical families. St. Justin wrote to the pagan emperor Antoninus Pius (138-161) around the year 155, explaining what Christians did:

On the day we call the day of the sun, all who dwell in the city or country gather in the same place.

The memoirs of the apostles and the writings of the prophets are read, as much as time permits.

When the reader has finished, he who presides over those gathered admonishes and challenges them to imitate these beautiful things.

Then we all rise together and offer prayers for ourselves . . .and for all others, wherever they may be, so that we may be found righteous by our life and actions, and faithful to the commandments, so as to obtain eternal salvation.

When the prayers are concluded we exchange the kiss.

Then someone brings bread and a cup of water and wine mixed

together to him who presides over the brethren.

He takes them and offers praise and glory to the Father of the universe, through the name of the Son and of the Holy Spirit and for a considerable time he gives thanks (in Greek: *eucharistian*) that we have been judged worthy of these gifts.

When he has concluded the prayers and thanksgivings, all present give voice to an acclamation by saying: 'Amen.'

When he who presides has given thanks and the people have responded, those whom we call deacons give to those present the "eucharisted" bread, wine and water and take them to those who are absent.

St. Justin goes on to point out their belief that the bread and wine of the Eucharist are actually the body and blood of Jesus. Justin writes:

We call this food Eucharist; ... For not as common bread nor common drink do we receive these; but since Jesus Christ our Savior was made incarnate by the word of God and had both flesh and blood for our salvation, so too, as we have been taught, the food which has been made into the Eucharist by the Eucharistic prayer set down by Him, and by the change of which our blood and flesh is nourished, is both the flesh and blood of that incarnated Jesus.[1]

The early Christians met on Sunday, read out loud as much scripture as time allowed, had a homily, prayers of the faithful, the sign of peace the kiss, and then mixed wine and water and over this and bread a prayer of thanksgiving was said after which the Eucharist was given to those present and taken to those who were absent. All of this is still done today in the Mass.. Thus when we worship at Mass we are not only standing with our friends and family but we are also worshiping with the very first Christians who walked with Jesus in the Mass.

---

[1] William A. Jurgens, The Faith of the Early Fathers (Collegeville, Minnesota: The Liturgical Press, 1970), Vol. I, p. 55.

⌘

3 THE WALK BEGINS

Our walk with Jesus begins before we even approach the church. The Catholic Church recommends that we fast for at least one hour before Mass and in earlier times the recommendation was twelve hours or more. The fast is not only a fast from food. It is also a fast from all the distractions of this world such as television and the Internet that can draw our thoughts away from Jesus.

Why would the Church make this recommendation? All journeys of significance require preparation. Moses withdrew to Mount Sinai and fasted for forty days before leading the Israelites to the promise land. Throughout the Bible fasting has been recommended over and over again as a means for spiritual preparation.

Most importantly Jesus fasted for forty days in the desert before he started his ministry. He was tempted by the devil to use his powers to have food, power and wealth. However, with the help of scripture, he was able to reject the temptations of this world. Jesus is our model in all situations and our goal in life is to be like him. Thus we too should fast.

What are we to do during this time? Jesus used scripture to help him resist temptations as he was fasting. Reading the account of Jesus' fast is a good beginning. Then reading your favorite passages would be next. This is also a good time to pray and talk with Jesus. Ask him how it felt to fast and to be tempted. Tell him how you feel at this moment and what tempts you. You two have something in common to talk about.

Of course family life often makes this time of preparation difficult. Getting small children ready for church and keeping a calm joyous atmosphere and getting to church on time are no small tasks. Just getting everyone ready a little earlier is a start. Sometimes parents can spell each other for a little quiet time before mass.

What if you give in to temptation and break your fast before church? You would not be the first to do so. After all you are only human. Remember how Jesus asked Peter to stay awake for only one hour while he prayed in the Garden of Gethsemane only to find him asleep. The different things that the Catholic Church asks us to do such as this one-hour fast or abstaining from meat on Fridays during Lent are not rules that condemn us when we break them. They are like our mothers' request for us to eat our vegetables because they know that they are good for our health. In a similar way the Church knows that what she requests is good for our spiritual health.

So what if you totally blow the fast before Mass? I would bet that when we have fallen Jesus, with a twinkle in his eye, gives us a hand to get up while he whispers in our ear "I have plans for you. Come."

⌘

4 THE ASCENSION

Every Catholic Church in the world has a font at the entrance with water in it that Catholics dip their fingers in and make the sign of the cross as they enter. The water, known as Holy Water, is to remind us of baptism. At that brief moment you are at the Ascension and you hear Christ say "Go therefore and make disciples of all the nations, baptizing them in the name of the Father and of the Son and of the Holy Spirit, teaching them to observe all that I have commanded you; and behold, I am with you always, to the close of the age" (Matthew 28:19-20).

Christ's last words speak of the Father, the Son and the Holy Spirit and baptism and making disciples of all nations. When Catholics make the sign of the cross they remember Jesus' words and say to themselves " Father, Son and Holy Spirit." This sign of the cross is an outward sign and is a simple but powerful gesture that may in a small way help spread the gospel as Jesus commanded.

However one might reasonably ask why does the Catholic Church want to remind everyone about baptism as they go to mass? It is because baptism is when we become the sons and daughters of God through adoption. Baptism then is essentially birth into God's family and it is then that Catholics are born again. To be adopted by God, Paul tells us, is the reason Jesus came.

"But when the time had fully come, God sent forth his Son, born of woman, born under the law, to redeem those who were under the law, so that we might receive adoption as sons. And because you are sons, God has sent the Spirit of his son into our hearts, crying, "Abba! Father!" So through God you are no longer a slave but a son, and if a son then an heir." (Galatians 4:4-7).

The importance of baptism is seen throughout the scriptures. Jesus began his ministry by being baptized and his last words are about baptism. Paul, whole households and every convert to Christ in the Bible are baptized as soon as they decided to become Christians. Peter tells us that baptism saves us (I Peter 3:21).

When Jesus was baptized a voice came down from heaven saying, "This is my beloved Son, with whom I am well pleased" (Matthew 3:17). At every baptism God is saying that this infant, child or adult is his son or daughter with whom he is well pleased.

Children enter their families at birth and as an infant are full members of their families and so it is in the Catholic Church and that is why infants are baptized. Infants are given the gift of faith at baptism and grow up in faith. They are also given free will and like the prodigal son they can choose to leave the faith when they grow up. However our Father, like the father in the parable, is always waiting for them with open arms to return.

So when you make the sign of the cross with Holy Water you are reminded of baptism. The wetness you feel on your forehead reminds you of how it felt on Jesus' forehead and on your own forehead when you were baptized. And for an instant you are with Jesus at his baptism and you are reminded that you are a son or daughter of God.

⌘

5 HOLY GROUND

In the bible when God was present physically the surroundings were holy. Since God is present physically in the Eucharist the church is a holy place. We might wonder how we should act in a holy place. God told Moses what to do as he approached the burning bush. "Remove your sandals from your feet, for the place where you stand is holy ground" (Exodus 3:5). We are thus with Moses as we enter to worship and we need instructions. Psalm 95:6 comes to our aid. "O come, let us worship and bow down, let us kneel before the Lord, our Maker!" (Psalm 95:6). So Catholics bow down by genuflecting on one knee and then enter the pew and kneel. Paul also gives us guidance when he says, "At the name of Jesus every knee should bend" (Philippians 2:10).

When we are kneeling we are usually kneeling with friends or family or church members but we are also kneeling with Jesus as knelt in the garden and with Stephen when he knelt and prayed at his martyrdom and with Paul in Ephesus and with all the Christians who have knelt and prayed throughout the last two thousand years. It is a time of private prayer before the Mass and our prayers join in with all those who throughout the world are also kneeling.

As we are kneeling and looking up at Jesus on the cross we may realize that we are also with someone else at the foot of the cross and that is Mary, Jesus' mother. Mary occupies a special place in the hearts of Catholics and here it might be a good time to say a few words about Mary.

Mary first of all shows us the importance God places on motherhood. Jesus could have just appeared but instead he chose to have a mother and a mother's love. Jesus loved and honored his mother making Mary the most loved and honored mother ever. Catholics believe that Jesus wants Mary to be our spiritual mother and that Mary loves each one of us as our mother. That is why Catholics believe that what Jesus said on the cross was meant for all of us, not just for our brother the apostle John. " When Jesus saw his mother and the disciple there whom he loved, he said to his mother, "Woman, behold, your son. "Then he said to the disciple, "Behold, your mother." And from that hour the disciple took her into his home" (John 19:26-27).

Catholics know that Mary is human but also the chosen mother of God. Catholics do not pray to Mary as they pray to God but they ask Mary to pray for them just as they ask others to pray for them. In their request for Mary's prayer Catholics also like to pray the scriptures and thus recite what the angel Gabriel said to Mary and what her cousin Elizabeth said when she saw Mary. These scriptures make up the well-known Hail Mary.

Hail Mary, full of grace, the Lord is with thee,

Blessed art thou among women,

and blessed is the fruit of thy womb, Jesus.

Holy Mary, Mother of God,

Pray for us sinners, now and at the hour of our death.

Mary was the very first Christian and her example serves as a model for all Christians. She loved Jesus and remained faithful to him to the very end. Her devotion both as a mother and as a follower has continued to inspire Christians for all times.

⌘

6 A JOYFUL NOISE

Psalm 95 says:

" Let us come into his presence with thanksgiving; Let us make a joyful noise to him with songs of praise!" (Psalm 95:2)

And thus the Mass starts with a joyful song as the entrance procession begins. The priest follows an altar boy or girl who carries a bronze pole with a crucifix at the top.

The crucifix on the pole takes us back over three thousand years to a time when the Israelites were wandering in the desert and a strange event occurred. Snakes began biting the Israelites and Moses asked God for help and God answered.

"And the LORD said to Moses, "Make a saraph and mount it on a pole, and if anyone who has been bitten looks at it, he will recover." Moses accordingly made a bronze serpent and mounted it on a pole, and whenever anyone who had been bitten by a serpent looked at the bronze serpent, he recovered" (Numbers 21: 8-9).

To many this is seemingly a minor and unimportant Old Testament happening. However Jesus refers to it in relation to himself.

"And just as Moses lifted up the serpent in the desert, so must the Son of Man be lifted up, so that everyone who believes in him may have eternal life." (John 3:14-15).

As the ancient Israelites looked at the serpent we look at Christ on the cross for healing in our lives.

When the priest reaches the altar he will bow in respect to the

Eucharist in the Tabernacle and then he will address the congregation. He may say a few introductory remarks and then he will usually say, " The grace of our Lord Jesus Christ and the love of God and the fellowship of the Holy Spirit be with you all." The priest is saying what Paul said to the Corinthians (2 Corinthians 13:14). For a moment he is Paul and you are standing with the Corinthians and Paul is speaking to you. And the congregation will respond as possibly the Corinthians did, " And with your spirit."

⌘

7 FATHER FORGIVE ME

At this point in the Mass we are asked to admit to God, to others and to ourselves that we are sinful by saying together:

I confess to almighty God

and to you, my brothers and sisters,

that I have greatly sinned,

in my thoughts and in my words,

in what I done and in what I have failed to do,

through my fault, through my fault,

through my most grievous fault;

therefore I ask blessed Mary ever-Virgin,

all the Angels and Saints,

and you, my brothers and sisters,

to pray for me to the Lord our God.

Jesus talked a lot about sin and at this point on our journey with Jesus we are asked to reflect on our sin. Sin harms others and is a weight on us that over time destroys our lives and our relationship with

God and our family and friends. To be able to overcome sin we need both forgiveness and healing. God is ready to forgive our sins but we must ask for this forgiveness which means we need to recognize our individual sins and be sorry for them. And then as instructed in the Lord's Prayer we are to forgive those who sinned against us.

An important part of the healing process is the confession of our sins. James tells us, "Therefore, confess your sins to one another and pray for one another, that you may be healed" (James 5:16). As in all things we need some practical guidance here. All sin is bad but there are definitely different degrees of sin. While it would be good to confess all our sins including the most minor ones, the Catholic Church teaches that there are certain sins called mortal sins that must be confessed. The apostle John tells us about mortal sins and the non mortal sins that the Catholic Church calls venial. "There is sin which is mortal; I do not say that one is to pray for that. All wrongdoing is sin, but there is sin which is not mortal" (1 John 5:16-17).

If we were to compare sin to disease venial sin is like arthritis that cripples us while mortal sin is like a heart attack. When we commit mortal sin we are indeed like the prodigal son who chose to leave his father's house. It some ways it is not that easy to commit a mortal sin and you cannot do so without knowing it. The Catechism of the Catholic Church points out that there are three conditions that must be met in order for a sin to be mortal. : "Mortal sin is sin whose object is grave matter and which is also committed with full knowledge and deliberate consent."

Thus to commit a mortal sin we must be fully aware of its seriousness and we decide to deliberately to forsake God and his teaching. Once we have committed a mortal sin we are essentially on our spiritual deathbed and we need help. The good news is that God the father and great physician is always right there for us when we are ready. The prodigal son came to his father and confessed and so must we. The prodigal son needed to hear his father's words of acceptance just as did all the people whom Jesus forgave. We in our humanness also need to hear the healing words of forgiveness. That is why the Catholic Church believes that God wants us to go to a priest for confession. God forgives sins and speaks that forgiveness through the priest. It was in the upper room that Christ breathed on the apostles reminiscent of God breathing into Adam and said, "Receive the holy Spirit. Whose sins you forgive are forgiven them, and whose sins you retain are retained" (John 20:23). The priest also gives us guidance. He will tell us that if we are not sorry for our sins they cannot be forgiven thus helping us gain spiritual wisdom. He will give a penance after forgiveness that again helps us heal from the effects of sin. In past times penances were severe but now consist of mainly of prayers and devotions.

Now, after we have joined with the others in the Mass admitting our sinfulness, it is time to ask for God's unending mercy.

⌘

8 A FATHER'S MERCY

There were three instances when Jesus was asked for his mercy. A Canaanite woman asked for mercy for herself and her daughter who was possessed by a demon. A man asked mercy for his son who was an epileptic and two blind men asked mercy for themselves. We are now standing with all those who asked Jesus for mercy and with the priest's guidance we too will ask for his mercy.

The priest will say, "Lord, have mercy." And then the congregation will say in unison, "Lord, have mercy." The priest will then say, "Christ, have mercy." The congregation will repeat, "Christ, have mercy." And finally the priest will say again, "Lord, have mercy" and the congregation will again say, "Lord, have mercy."

In some churches the priest and congregation will say or sing the pleas for mercy in Greek. They will say, "Kyrie, eleison" for "Lord, have mercy" and "Christe, eleison" for "Christ, have mercy." When Jesus lived Greek was the language of the world outside of Israel. Greek was the language of the early Christians as Christianity spread though out the known world. Thus when we say, "Christe, eleison", we are standing with the earliest Christians and speaking the exact same words that they spoke as they asked for God's mercy.

We ask for mercy three times for God is three in one and we also remember those who asked Jesus for mercy. We ask for mercy because we need God's mercy. We ask for mercy because it restores our right relationship with our Lord. Our cries for mercy are our testimony of faith. We would not ask for mercy if we did not believe that Jesus was indeed our Lord.

Thus it is at this time in the Mass that we again enter the scriptures and stand by Jesus. It is also a time in which we feel great hope within our hearts.

⌘

9 HEAVENLY VOICES

At this time in the Mass we join our voices with voices throughout the Bible in praising and thanking God because he is so merciful. The voices we join include the angels in the heavens at Bethlehem, the psalmist, John the Baptist, those in heavenly worship in Revelation and many more as we say the Gloria.

Glory to God in the highest,

and on earth peace to people of good will.

We praise you,

we bless you,

we adore you,

we glorify you,

we give you thanks for your great glory,

Lord God, heavenly King,

O God, almighty Father.

Lord Jesus Christ, Only Begotten Son,

Lord God, Lamb of God, Son of the Father,

you take away the sins of the world,

have mercy on us;

you take away the sins of the world,

receive our prayer;

you are seated at the right hand of the Father,

have mercy on us.

For you alone are the Holy One,

you alone are the Lord,

you alone are the Most High,

Jesus Christ,

With the Holy Spirit,

in the glory of God the Father.

Amen.

⌘

10 BEAUTIFUL THINGS

St. Justin tells us that in the worship of the first Christians as much scripture was read as time allowed and then "he who presides over those gathered admonishes and challenges them to imitate these beautiful things." After a brief period of silence, followed by a short, simple and beautiful opening prayer, the Liturgy of the Word begins with a reading of scripture, the "beautiful things."

The scripture usually consists of an Old Testament passage followed by a psalm which is usually sung as was originally intended, then a reading from one of the letters in the New Testament followed by a reading from the Gospel. When the Gospel is read everyone stands to hear the actual words of Jesus.

The readings are coordinated to show their relationship to each other and are planned so that essentially the entire Bible is read every three years. Every Catholic Church in the world reads the same scriptures at each Mass and thus Catholics contemplate them and pray over them in a worldwide unity.

Reading aloud as much of the scriptures as possible in Mass was very important to the first Christians. The scriptures had been read in the synagogues for hundreds of years and the early Christians continued this custom. The Passover meal was celebrated only once a year but when the Christians began to worship outside of the synagogue they combined at each service the scripture readings of the synagogue with the new Passover meal that Jesus had instituted, the Eucharist. Christians also read aloud the writings of Paul, the apostles and others such as St. Luke as they became available. When St. John wrote the book of Revelations he said, "Blessed is the one who reads aloud and blessed are those who listen to this prophetic message and heed what is written in it" (Revelation 1:3). Paul wrote to the Colossians instructing them to read his letters in church. "And when this letter is read before you, have it read also in the church of the Laodiceans, and you yourselves read the one from Laodicea" (Colossians 4:16). Again to the Thessalonians he wrote, "I adjure you by the Lord that this letter be read to all the brothers" (I Thessalonians 5:27).

The Word of God and the message that it brings are indeed beautiful things. When we listen to scripture we are with Christ when he read in the temple and we are with the first Christians in their worship. We also encounter Christ himself in scripture. John tells us, "In the beginning was the Word, and the Word was with God, and the Word was God." (John 1:1) "And the Word became flesh and made his dwelling among us, and we saw his glory, the glory as of the Father's only Son, full of grace and truth." (John 1:14) Paul writes, "in receiving the word of God from hearing us, you received not a human word but, as it truly is, the word of God." (I Thessalonians 2:13).

After the readings the priest or deacon speaks for Christ and explains how the scriptures speak to us and how they apply to our daily lives. And they in essence challenge each one of us to "to imitate these beautiful things."

⌘

11 I BELIEVE

After the reading of the scriptures in the Mass there is a short period of silence and then everyone stands and confesses their belief by reciting the Nicene Creed. At this time Jesus is asking us the same question he asked Martha when he said, "Do you believe this?" (John 11:26). Paul tells us in Romans that we must confess with our lips that "Jesus is Lord" and so at this time we confess our faith.

The Nicene Creed is an important summary of the belief of the Catholic Church. The word creed comes from the Latin word *credo*, which means, "I believe." The Nicene Creed has been the basis of the Christian faith for almost 1700 years and when we recite it we are joined with all Christians throughout the centuries in our common belief.

The Catholic Church put the Nicene Creed together in A.D. 325 at the Council of Nicea. It not only served as a summary of the Christian faith but it also helped save the Christian faith from heresies that threatened the faith as we know it today. There were a very large number of Christians who for many years followed the teachings of Arius who taught that Jesus was not God but was a man made by God like Adam and then chosen for a special role. The creed addressed and put an end to this heresy stating that Jesus was "the Only Begotten Son of God, born of the Father before all ages, God from God, Light from Light, true God from true God, begotten, not made..."

Another heresy that many held that threatened the faith was the belief that Jesus was never really human, but only appeared to be human. The underlying assumption here was that creation and our bodies are not good and thus Jesus could never have been human with a human body. This heresy was called *Docetism.* The creed countered this by stating Jesus "was incarnate of the Virgin Mary and became man."

      Following the creed are the Prayers of the Faithful where we, like the first Christians "offer prayers for ourselves . . .and for all others."

The Nicene Creed

    I believe in one God,

    the Father almighty,

    maker of heaven and earth,

    of all things visible and invisible.

    I believe in one Lord Jesus Christ,

    the Only Begotten Son of God,

    born of the Father before all ages.

    God from God, Light from Light,

    true God from true God,

    begotten, not made, consubstantial with the Father;

    through him all things were made.

    For us men and for our salvation

    he came down form heaven,

    and by the Holy Spirit was incarnate of the Virgin Mary,

    and became man.

For our sake he was crucified under Pontius Pilate,

he suffered death and was buried,

and rose again on the third day

in accordance with the Scriptures.

He ascended into heaven

and is seated at the right hand of the Father.

He will come again in glory

to judge the living and the dead

and his kingdom will have no end.

I believe in the Holy Spirit, the Lord, the giver of life,

who proceeds from the Father and the Son,

who with the Father and the Son is adored and glorified,

who has spoken through the prophets.

I believe in one, holy, catholic and apostolic Church,

I confess one Baptism for the forgiveness of sins

and I look forward to the resurrection of the dead

and the life of the world to come. Amen.

⌘

12 THE ROAD TO EMMAUS

As we walk with Jesus in the Mass we are also walking with him and the disciples on the road to Emmaus where we see the form or structure of the Mass that we continue to follow today. When Jesus joined the disciples as they went to Emmaus they did not recognize him. They expressed their sorrow over the death of Jesus and then recounted the reports they had heard of his resurrection. Jesus began with scripture and the disciples reported that their hearts were burning as he spoke. "And beginning with Moses and all the prophets, be interpreted to them in all the Scriptures the things concerning himself." (Luke 24:27).

Jesus then sat with them and then "he took bread and blessed and broke it, and gave it to them." (Luke 24:30). Their eyes were opened and they recognized Jesus and they went back to the apostles and recalled "how he was known to them in the breaking of the bread." (Luke 24:35).

The breaking of the bread was not simply the breaking of a piece of bread, it referred to the Eucharist at the last supper when Jesus " took bread, and blessed, and broke it." (Mark 14:22). Paul tells us, "The cup of blessing that we bless, is it not a participation in the blood of Christ? The bread that we break, is it not a participation in the body of Christ?" (I Corinthians 10:16). The disciples devoted themselves to this "breaking of the bread." St. Luke tells us in Acts 2:42, "They devoted themselves to the teaching of the apostles, and to the communal life, to the breaking of the bread and to the prayers." In Acts 2:46 St. Luke states, "Every day they devoted themselves to meeting together in the temple area and to breaking bread in their homes." Again in Acts 20:7, "On the first day of the week when we gathered to break bread, Paul spoke to them because he was going to leave on the next day. "

Thus on that first meeting with Jesus on the road to Emmaus

scripture was interpreted followed by the Eucharist, or the breaking of the bread. So it is with our Mass. The first part of the Mass is the Liturgy of the Word where scripture is read and interpreted and the second part of the Mass is the Liturgy of the Eucharist where the bread is broken. Liturgy refers to the form or structure of the worship. Like the first disciples our hearts burn with the opening of the scriptures and we recognize Jesus in the breaking of the bread.

⌘

13 THE WORK OF HUMAN HANDS

The beginning of the Liturgy of the Eucharist begins with the bringing of the offerings and bread and wine to the altar. These gifts are directly or indirectly the work of human hands emphasizing the importance of human work and the fact that they are offered to God emphasizes that as important as they are, God is more important. The priest will then mix a small amount of water with the wine symbolizing the humanity and divinity of Christ and our own humanity as we receive the body of Christ. The priest will offer a prayer of preparation over these gifts again putting all this in its proper perspective. The prayer begins a dialogue between the priest and the people that will continue throughout the Liturgy of the Eucharist drawing the congregation into and making them an essential part of the worship.

Priest: Blessed are you, Lord God of all creation,

for through your goodness we have received

the bread we offer you:

 fruit of the earth and work of human hands,

It will become for us the bread of life.

People: Blessed be God for ever.

Priest: Blessed are you, Lord God of all creation,

for through your goodness we have received

the wine we offer you:

fruit of the vine and work of human hands

It will become our spiritual drink.

People: Blessed be God for ever.

Priest: Pray, brethren (brothers and sisters),

that my sacrifice and yours

may be acceptable to God,

the almighty Father.

People: May the Lord accept the sacrifice at your hands

for the praise and glory of his name,

for our good

and the good of all his holy Church.

After this the priest says a simple prayer of thanks over the gifts. Like the opening prayer, the prayer over the gifts differs at each Mass and again is brief, simple and beautiful.

⌘

14 GIVING THANKS

When Jesus instituted the Eucharist at the Last Supper he gave thanks over the bread and wine before giving it to his apostles. We do not know exactly what he said at this time but most surely his words remained in the hearts of the apostles and greatly influenced the subsequent Eucharistic prayers in the early church and throughout the centuries. Eucharist means thanksgiving and St. Justin tells us of the prayer of thanks over the bread and wine in the worship of the first Christians. In 155 AD St. Justin writes:

Then someone brings bread and a cup of water and wine mixed together to him who presides over the brethren.

He takes them and offers praise and glory to the Father of the universe, through the name of the Son and of the Holy Spirit and for a considerable time he gives thanks (in Greek: *eucharistian*) that we have been judged worthy of these gifts.

When he has concluded the prayers and thanksgivings, all present give voice to an acclamation by saying: 'Amen.'

Thus we are now with Christ and the apostles in the upper room and we are also with the early Christians as the priest begins to pray one of four Eucharistic prayers over the bread and wine. The priest will begin by asking the congregation to lift up their spirits as was the spirit of St. John lifted up in revelation. He will then give thanks and praise and he will ask the Holy Spirit to descend on the bread and wine and make them holy so that they will become the Body and Blood of Jesus Christ.

The priest then will act in the place of Christ at the Last Supper when he instructed his apostles to do this in remembrance of him. He will hold up the bread and wine that is about to consecrated and say:

For on the night he was betrayed he himself took bread, and, giving you thanks, he said the blessing, broke the bread and gave it to his disciples, saying:

Take this all of you, and eat of it,

For this is my Body,

Which will be given up for you.

In a similar way, when supper was ended, He took the chalice, And giving you thanks, he said the blessing, And gave the chalice to his disciples, saying:

Take this all of you, and drink from it,

For this is the chalice of my Blood,

The Blood of the new and

   Eternal covenant,

Which will be poured out for you and

   For many

For the forgiveness of sins.

Do this in memory of me.

The bread and wine are now the Body and Blood of Christ. This is a sacred moment in the Mass when time has no meaning. You are at the Last Supper with Jesus and the disciples and Jesus is talking directly to you. And along with the disciples you now understand what Jesus meant when he said, "I am the living bread that came down from heaven; whoever eats this bread will live forever; and the bread that I will give is my flesh for the life of the world." (John 6:51).

After the institution of the Eucharist the priest continues with praise and thanksgiving to God and prays for all of us and for the salvation of the whole world. He will also give thanks for the prayers of Mary, the mother of Jesus and all the heavenly saints who pray for us. He will ask God to guide his church on earth and he will pray for the pope, the bishops, all the clergy and his people on earth and he will pray that God will gather all the children on earth that have been scattered. He will also pray for all the departed.

⌘

15 THE PRAYER OF OUR LORD

The Lord's Prayer is considered a perfect prayer as it should be since it was given to us by Jesus himself. It begins powerfully with "Our Father". These simple words let us know that God is a father and that he is our father which means we, his children, are brothers and sisters to each other. Following this are seven petitions. The first three relate to God and the last four relate to ourselves.

At every Mass the priest invites all to say the Lord's Prayer together.

All: Our Father, who art in heaven,

hallowed be thy name;

thy kingdom come, thy will be done

on earth as it is in heaven.

Give us this day our daily bread,

and forgive us our trespasses,

as we forgive those who trespass against us;

and lead us not into temptation,

but deliver us from evil.

Priest: Deliver us, Lord, we pray, from every evil,

graciously grant peace in our days,

that, by the help of your mercy,

we may be always free from sin

and safe from all distress,

as we await the blessed hope

and the coming of our Savior, Jesus Christ.

All: For the kingdom, the power and the glory are yours now and forever.

⌘

16 PEACE BE WITH YOU

The priest will next ask everyone to offer each other a sign of peace as Jesus did to the apostles in the upper room. The sign of peace referred to as the "kiss" was part of the worship of the first Christians.

Priest: Lord Jesus Christ

who said to your Apostles:

Peace I leave you, my peace I give you,

look not on our sins,

but on the faith of your Church,

and graciously grant her peace and unity

in accordance with your will.

Who live and reign for ever and ever.

People: Amen.

Priest: The peace of the Lord be with you always.

People: And with your spirit.

Priest: Let us offer each other the sign of peace.

At this time everyone offers to all around them a sign of peace. Each person will usually say either "The peace of the Lord be with you" or simply "Peace be with you" as they kiss or hug their relatives and shake hands with others.

CARL TURNER

⌘

17 LAMB OF GOD

After the sign of peace the congregation sings what John the Baptist said when he saw Jesus walking.

Lamb of God, you take away the sins of the world, have mercy on us.

Lamb of God, you take away the sins of the world, grant us peace.

The priest will then elevate the consecrated bread and say:

> Behold the Lamb of God
>
> Behold him who takes away the sins of the world
>
> Blessed are those called to the supper of the Lamb.

The congregation will then reaffirm their faith in Jesus by saying what the Roman centurion said when Jesus was going to heal his servant:

> Lord, I am not worthy
>
> that you should enter under my roof,
>
> But only say the word
>
> and my soul shall be healed.

The congregation will then come forward and receive the Body and Blood of Christ and then return to their pew and kneel in prayer. This is a most sacred moment. Jesus has loved us so much that he has given all of himself to us and we hear him say, "He who eats my flesh and drinks my blood abides in me, and I in him" (John 6:56).

If there are those who are ill or confined someone will take the Eucharist to them.

After all have received Christ there is a period of silence. Then the priest will say:

> May almighty God bless you:
>
> the Father, and the Son, and the Holy Spirit.

Any remaining Blood of Christ which is in the form of wine will be consumed by the servers, deacon or priest and any remaining Body of Christ in the form of bread will be reverently placed in the tabernacle.

⌘

18 ITE MISSA EST

The word Mass comes from the Latin words, *Ite missa est*, that were said at the end of Mass. *Ite missa est* means "Go, it is sent" meaning "Go, the (congregation) is sent." Mass comes from the word missa.

Thus the Mass itself means not an ending, but a sending forth of the children of God into the world to love and serve the Lord. It is at this final part of the Mass that a deacon or priest will give one of several concluding dismissals:

Deacon/Priest: Go in peace, glorifying the Lord by your life.

All: Thanks be to God

.

⌘

19 I AM WITH YOU

Now that the Mass is ended our physical walk with Jesus has ended but our spiritual walk continues as we go forth to love God and our neighbors and to spread the gospel. The Mass is like time travel. We are taken back to the time of Jesus and we enter scripture and walk with him just as the disciples did. As we leave Mass we are back where we started at the ascension and we can hear Jesus say, "and behold, I am with you always, to the close of the age."

⌘

20 INCENSE, HOLY WATER AND BLESSINGS

The basic structure of the walk with Jesus, known as the Mass, is the same in all Masses all over the world. Different languages and music will be used depending on the local culture. Special Masses such as Masses on Holy days or for other special occasions such as weddings, funerals and ordinations will employ different Eucharistic prayers and other prayers. However the basic structure of the Mass is preserved.

There are also two additions that a priest may add to the Mass for special occasions and these are the use of incense and the sprinkling of Holy Water on the congregation to impart a special blessing.

Incense is placed in what is called a censor that is held by a chain and gently swung around the altar, the scriptures or the congregation. It is also used in special processions and at funerals. The smoke of the burning incense gently rises accompanied by a pleasant fragrance.

The use of incense dates back to Moses and beyond. God gave instructions to Moses to build an altar for burning incense. "For burning incense you shall make an altar of acacia wood" (Exodus 30:1). God also gave instructions on the use of incense. "On it Aaron shall burn fragrant incense. Morning after morning, when he prepares the lamps and again in the evening twilight, when he lights the lamps, he shall burn incense" (Exodus 30:7-8).

Incense is used over and over again throughout the Old Testament. It is also mentioned in the New Testament. Zechariah, the father of John the Baptist, was chosen to burn incense in the temple when the angel of the Lord appeared to him. "He was chosen by lot to enter the sanctuary of the Lord to burn incense. Then, when the whole assembly of the people was praying outside at the hour of the incense offering, the angel of the Lord appeared to him, standing at the right of the altar of incense" (Luke 1:9-11).

Most importantly incense is used in the heavenly worship that St. John witnessed and wrote about in Revelation. "Another angel came and stood at the altar, holding a gold censer. He was given a great quantity of incense to offer, along with the prayers of the holy ones, on the gold altar that was before the throne. The smoke of the incense along with the prayers of the holy ones went up before God from the hand of the angel" (Revelation 8:3-4).

Incense then represents the prayers of all the faithful that rise to God from their hearts, which have been set on fire by God's love. The use of incense not only reminds us of our prayers to God but also connects us with all those throughout the whole Bible and those in heavenly worship who have used incense.

The sprinkling of Holy water on the congregation also has its roots in the Old Testament. A hyssop branch was used to sprinkle specially prepared water on an unclean person, their family and their tent as an act of purification.

> For anyone who is thus unclean, ashes from the sin offering shall be put in a vessel, and spring water shall be poured on them. Then a man who is clean shall take some hyssop, dip it in this water, and sprinkle it on the tent and on all the vessels and persons that were in it, or on him who touched a bone, a slain person or other dead body, or a grave (Numbers 19:17-18).

Holy water is placed at the entrance of all Catholic Churches to remind all those who enter there the importance of baptism at which time God adopted them as sons and daughters, saved them and cleansed them of original sin. When the priest on special occasions sprinkles the congregation with Holy Water it is to remind them of baptism and to impart a special blessing upon them.

Blessings in the Catholic Church are very important and it would be good to explore what blessings mean to Catholics. The Catechism of the Catholic Church defines blessings in the following way. "Blessing is a divine and life-giving action, the source of which is the Father; his blessing is both word and gift" (CCC 1078). In one sense everything from God is a blessing. "From the beginning until the end of time the whole of God's work is a blessing" (CCC 1079). "From the very beginning God blessed all living beings, especially man and woman" (CCC 1080).

Thus blessings are a continuation of God's "life-giving action" to man. God blesses us everyday. However when a priest uses his authority to impart a blessing it is a special moment when God shows his love for us. It is much like when a parent hugs his or her child. The parent loves and gives to the child everyday. But the hug has a special meaning for the child. Blessings are like that. They are a caress by God, an embrace that warms our hearts as we are reminded of God's love for us.

Thus the sprinkling of the Holy Water upon us is God's blessing of love and incense reminds us of our prayers that are a response to God's blessing.

CARL TURNER

OUTLINE OF THE MASS

Fasting for one hour

Entering the Sanctuary – The Ascension

Genuflecting and kneeling – Holy Ground

The Entrance Procession – A Joyful Noise

The Greeting

Penitential Act – Father Forgive Me

Lord Have Mercy – A Father's Mercy

Gloria – Heavenly Voices

Prayer

The Liturgy of the Word

   Reading of Scripture – Beautiful Things

   Profession of Faith – I Believe

   Prayer of the Faithful

The Liturgy of the Eucharist

   Presentation and Preparation of the Gifts – The Work of Human Hands

   Prayer

   The Eucharistic Prayer – Giving Thanks

   The Prayer of Our Lord

   Sign of Peace – Peace Be With You

Lamb of God

Communion

Concluding Rites – I Am With You

RECOMMENDED RESOURCES

The Bible

The Catechism of the Catholic Church and Compendium: Catechism of the Catholic Church

> The Catechism of the Catholic Church is an excellent summary of the Catholic Faith. The Compendium of the Catechism of the Catholic Church written by the United States Conference of Catholic Bishops is a very good introduction to the main contents of the Catechism.

Catholicism by Father Robert Barron.

> This is an amazing ten part video series. Father Barron takes you on an around the world adventure as he explains the Catholic faith. The Catholic faith comes alive as you see Catholics in all cultures worship and serve God. The scenery and the cathedrals are breathtaking. The video quality and music are excellent. One whole episode is devoted to explaining the Mass. This can be purchased at his website: www.wordonfire.org/

The Lamb's Supper: The Mass As Heaven On Earth. Doubleday, 1999 by Dr. Scott Hahn.

> Dr. Hahn presents a very insightful and inspiring look at the Mass and explains its amazing connection with Revelation.

The Faith of the Early Fathers. The Liturgical Press, 1970 by William A Jurgens.

This is a well-organized collection of the actual writings of the early fathers.

ABOUT THE AUTHOR

Carl Turner is a retired pediatrician who with his wife Diane has been involved in faith formation working with both adults and teenagers at St. Joseph's Catholic Church in Marshall Texas for
over twenty years.

Made in the USA
Lexington, KY
21 March 2017